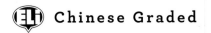 **Chinese Graded**

ELI Chinese Graded Reade
of texts and original stories ....
culture and civilization. It is ideal for
readers of all ages. The books are carefully
edited and contain a wealth of activities
and numerous illustrations to capture the
essence of the topics. The books include
Chinese-Pinyin-English glossaries to
promote and guide comprehension.

Chiara Perinot - Chen Haiyan

中国成语故事
Stories of Chinese Proverbs

Illustrated by Silvia Nencini

Chinese Graded Readers

中国成语故事
Stories of Chinese Proverbs
Chiara Perinot - Chen Haiyan

Illustrations
Silvia Nencini

ELI Chinese Graded Readers
Founder and Series Editors
Paola Accattoli, Grazia Ancillani, Daniele Garbuglia (Art Director)

Graphic Design
Sergio Elisei

Layout
Davide Elisei

Language Revision
Laura Severini

Production Manager
Francesco Capitano

© 2020 ELI s.r.l.
P.O. Box 6
62019 Recanati MC
Italy
T +39 071750701
F +39 071977851
info@elionline.com
www.elionline.com

Typeset in 11,5 / 15 Monotype Dante

Printed in Italy by Tecnostampa – Pigini Group Printing Division –
Loreto, Trevi (Italia) – ERC204.01

ISBN 978-88-536-3331-6

First edition: December 2020

www.eligradedreaders.com

目录 Contents

These icons indicate the parts of the story that are recorded. **start** ▶ **stop** ■

1. 有志竟成

▶2   在城市运动会上，有人高兴<u>地</u>大叫了起来："我<u>终于</u>完成了！"那是安娜，她刚刚跑完了马拉松比赛，还拿了第一名。这时，她<u>正在</u>回答<u>记者</u>的问题。

记者：你觉得怎么样？

安娜：我很累，可是很<u>满意</u>！

记者：你练习跑步<u>多久</u>了？

安娜：<u>快</u>三年了，今天是第一次参加马拉松，没想到能跑完，还跑出了好成绩。

记者：<u>才</u>三年？

安娜：是的，因为我以前不喜欢运动，工作很忙，也没时间。

记者：你做什么工作呢？

安娜：我是<u>护士</u>，下班后回家带小孩，跟我的小马可一起玩游戏、讲故事。

记者：那你是怎么开始跑步的呢？

安娜：有一次跟马可的体育老师聊天，我说经常觉得很累，影响工作。他说跑步可以让人快乐，我决定试一下。

地 de *determining verbal particle*
终于 zhōngyú *eventually, finally*
正在 zhèngzài *gerund marker*
记者 jìzhě *journalist*

满意 mǎnyì *satisfied*
多久 duōjiǔ *how long*
快 kuài *fast, about to*
才 cái *only, just*
护士 hùshi *nurse*

早上六点起床，到附近公园一边听音乐，一边跑步，慢慢就习惯了，对跑步也越来越感兴趣，现在刮风下雨我都会去。

记者：你一个人跑吗？

安娜：开始的时候周一到周五一个人跑，一到周末还找朋友和同事一起去。后来，我还告诉我的病人，要多做运动，努力锻炼身体才会健康，所以跑步成了我们的共同爱好。

记者：你为什么要参加这次比赛？

安娜：为了我儿子马可，他害怕困难，我想让他明白，有志竟成，只要努力，不容易的事情也可以做到。

记者：你会一直跑下去吗？

安娜：会的，跑步对我影响很大，对身体健康也有帮助，我希望有越来越多人参加这个运动。■

你来猜！Try to guess: what is the moral of this story? Is there a similar proverb in English?

一边。。。一边。。。 yībiān··· yībiān··· *indicates two actions happening at the same time* (一边 VERB 一边 VERB)
越来越 yuè lái yuè *more and more + adjective / verb*

周 zhōu *week*
努力 nǔlì *willing, keen*
健康 jiànkāng *health, healthy*
害怕 hàipà *to be afraid/scared*
困难 kùnnan *difficulty*

语言点 A closer look

1 "有人高兴地大叫了起来" The particle 地 de

The particle 地 is a determining verb particle which is positioned between an adjective and a verb: ADJ + 地 + VERB.
The adjective, in front of the verb and followed by 地, indicates the way the action is carried out, taking on the function of an adverb.

- 高兴地走 To walk happily
- 慢慢地学习 To study slowly

> **注意 !**
>
> This character can be pronounced in two ways:
> 地　de is a particle
> 　　dì means *earth*, as in 地球, *world globe*

2 "有人高兴地大叫了起来" Verb + 起来 qǐlái

In this sentence, the structure of a verb followed by 起来 can be translated as *to start to* + verb.

- 他马上高兴起来了。 He immediately cheered up. (He started to feel happy.)
- 冬天的时候天很早就黑起来。 In winter it gets dark early. (It starts to turn black early.)

> **注意 !**
>
> The structure VERB + 起来 refers to a compound directional verb. [→ p. 35]

3 "今天是第一次参加马拉松，没想到能跑完，还跑出了好成绩。" Resultative verbs

跑完 and 跑出 are resultative verbs, according to the V1 + V2 method where V2 represents the result of V1, which is the main verb.

- 她跑完了马拉松。 She completed the marathon. (She ran and she finished the marathon.)
  The verb 完 *to finish* indicated the result of 跑 *to run*.
- 我弟弟打烂了花瓶。 My little brother broke the vase.
- 打 *to hit* and 烂 *to be broken* → 打烂, to hit until it results in breaking.

9

4 "那你是怎么开始跑步的呢？"

The structure 是。。。的 shì... de

The structure 是。。。的 is used to highlight a part of the sentence, just like a highlighter pen! 是 can be omitted, but 的 must always be included and always at the end of the sentence. It is usually used in sentences which talk about the past.

- 他是坐火车去上海的。 He went to Shanghai by train. (This highlights the fact that he went by train, and not a different means of transport.)
- 他是2004年出生的。 He was born in 2004. (This highlights the fact that he was born in 2004, and not a different year.)

小贴士

To understand if the 是。。。的 structure is used, we can try to take it out and see if the sentence makes sense without it.

成语中的成语 A proverb in a proverb

As well as proverbs, often formed by four characters, Chinese also has many sayings and expressions which, in turn, are made up of four characters called 俗语 súyǔ (figure of speech). In this story there is 刮风下雨 guāfēng xiàyǔ, which it could be translated as "with any type of weather conditions" or "there could be wind or there could be rain". You will find the proverbs in the following stories highlighted in orange.

Activities
练习

1 Guess the meaning of the following words.

猜猜生词的意思。

1 ☐ 带小孩   **a** to do exercise
2 ☐ 习惯   **b** to look after children
3 ☐ 周末   **c** weekend
4 ☐ 锻炼   **d** help
5 ☐ 帮助   **e** to get used to something

2 Answer the following questions.

回答以下问题。

1 为什么马可的妈妈开始锻炼跑步？
2 谁说服她跑步可以解决她很多问题？
3 她觉得跑步对她有好处吗？
4 她赢了这次马拉松以后还会继续跑步吗？为什么？

▶2 **3** Dictation: Listen to the recording and write the story in Chinese.

听写练习：认真听录音，然后把故事用汉字写下来。

4 Let's talk about you!

说说自己！

1 你是所谓的(so-called)沙发土豆还是喜欢参加各种各样的运动项目？
2 你喜欢跑步吗？为什么？
3 意大利最流行的运动项目是什么？中国的呢？

2. 画蛇添足

　　很久以前，楚国有一个有钱人，他买了一桶又好喝又贵的酒，然后请了很多朋友到他家里来做客，准备把好酒都给朋友喝。

　　参加他的宴会的人非常多。酒非常好喝，大家都喝得很开心。到差不多喝完，只剩下最后一杯的时候，大家都还想喝，但是到底给谁喝最后一杯呢？

　　这时有一个人想了个办法，对大家说：

　　"这样吧，咱们来比赛画蛇。谁先画好，又画得像，最后一杯酒就让谁喝。"

　　大家都同意了，就开始用树枝在地上画蛇。有一个人画得很快，用了几分钟时间就把蛇画好了。

　　他看到大家都还在画，就说："你们还没画好呀，你们真慢！你们看看我吧，我还来得及给蛇添上四只脚哩！"

蛇 shé *snake*
添 tiān *to add*
久 jiǔ *(a long) time*
楚国 Chǔ guó *The Chu Kingdom*
(770 B.C.-223 B.C.)
又...又... yòu... yòu... *both...and...*
准备 zhǔnbèi *to prepare, to get ready;*
准备 + verb *to get ready to do something*

宴会 yànhuì *banquet*
剩下 shèng xia *to stay*
咱们 zánmen *we (includes the spokesperson)*
像 xiàng *to resemble*
让 ràng *to let, to allow*
树枝 shùzhī *branch*
来得及 láidejí *to have (enough) time to do something*
哩 li *final particle* (similar to 呢 or 啦)

他一边说一边拿着最后一杯酒,一边喝一边又在地上给他之前画好的蛇添上脚。他还没把四只脚画完,就有另外一个人也把蛇画好了,还抢了他手里的酒杯,几口就把酒喝干了,对他说："你没见过蛇吗?蛇没有脚,你干嘛要给它画四只脚呢?你画的不是蛇,所以你不能喝这杯酒!第一个画好蛇的人是我,酒我来喝!"说完这句话,他把酒咕咚咕咚地喝完了。

"画蛇添足"这句成语就是从这个故事来的。意思是一个人做了多余的事,而且没有用处。

你来猜！Try to guess: what is the moral of this story? Is there a similar proverb in English?

注意！

The character 得 has three different meanings and pronunciations; do you know what they are?

1 得 ....   2 得 ....   3 得 ....

抢 qiǎng *to steal*
所以 suǒyǐ *so, therefore*
咕咚咕咚 gūdōng gūdōng *gulp*
(onomatopoeic sound of swallowing)

多余 duōyú *superfluous, extra*
用处 yòngchu *use*

14

语言点 A closer look

1 "请了很多朋友到他家里来做客，准备把好酒都给朋友喝。" **The preposition** 把 bǎ

In Chinese, we use the preposition 把 to place the object in front of the verb: subject + 把 + object + verb.
The object must be defined and known to the speakers. The verb can not be simple, and must be followed by another element, such as a directional, a resultative, or a modal 了.
- 他把我买的酒都喝完了。He has drunk all the wine that I bought.
- 请把客人叫出来。[→ p. 35] Please, ask all the guests to come outside.

2 "这样吧，咱们来比赛画蛇。谁先画好，又画得像，最后一杯酒就让谁喝。" **The structural particle** 得 de

The structural particle 得 is used to express the complement of degree, that is the way in which an action is carried out which is expressed by the verb: subject + verb + 得 + complement.
If there is an object, the structure of the sentence is: subject + object + verb + 得 + complement. In a negative sentence, the negation 不 comes before the complement.
- 他喝得很快。He drinks quickly.
- 他喝咖啡喝得很慢。He drinks the coffee slowly.
- 我妈妈做饭做得很好吃。My mum cooks very well. (very good)

3 "你没见过蛇吗？" **The aspect particle** 过 guo

We use the aspect particle 过 to talk about the experience of the verb in use. It comes after the verb which it refers to.
- 你吃过中国菜吗？Have you ever eaten Chinese food? (Have you, at least once in your life, had the experience of eating Chinese food?)
- 我去过很多地方，但是没(有)去过中国。I have been to a lot of places, but I have never been to China.

4 "咱们来比赛画蛇。" **A special use of** 来 lái

The verb 来, when it is followed by another verb, shows the intention or the request to do something.
- "谁来读生词?" "我来吧" "Who is going to read the new words?" "I'll read them."
- 我来介绍一下我的朋友。Let me introduce you to my friend.

Activities
练习

汉语怎么说？How do you say in Chinese?

How do you ask a friend what zodiac sign (Chinese sign) he is?

你 属 什么？   What sign are you?
Nǐ shǔ shénme?

我 属 蛇。   I'm the sign of the snake.
Wǒ shǔ shé.

1 There are 12 signs of the Chinese zodiac; try to match the words with the pictures.

12个生肖，你来搭配！

1 ☐ 鼠   4 ☐ 鸡   7 ☐ 兔   10 ☐ 马
2 ☐ 牛   5 ☐ 狗   8 ☐ 龙   11 ☐ 羊
3 ☐ 虎   6 ☐ 猪   9 ☐ 蛇   12 ☐ 猴

a

b

c

d

e

f

g

h

i

j

k

l

2 Now that you know the names of the animals, match them with the sounds they make.

给下面的动物叫声选择对应的图片。

1 □ 马   5 □ 青蛙   9 □ 羊

2 □ 猫   6 □ 牛   10 □ 鸽

3 □ 狗   7 □ 鸭

4 □ 鸡   8 □ 猪

a 咴儿   b 喵喵   c 汪汪   d 喔喔   e 呱呱

f 哞哞   g 嘎嘎   h 咕噜   i 咩咩   j 咕咕

Have you noticed that nearly all the characters have something in common? Why?

▶3 **3** Dictation: Listen to the recording and write the story in Chinese.

听写练习：认真听录音，然后把故事用汉字写下来。

Did you know...?

In Chinese cuisine there is a very famous dish which takes its name from the sound that a pig makes.

咕噜肉

Sweet and sour pork is a traditional Cantonese dish (粤菜) which is said to have been invented for the benefit of the foreigners who, during the 19th century, used to visit the coast of Southern China. This is because they really liked the sweet and sour ribs which were typical of the area, but they didn't appreciate the local custom of spitting out the bones.

The snake in Chinese mythology

The snake is one of the 12 signs of the Chinese zodiac and there are many sayings, proverbs and legends about this animal. But, in Chinese culture, how is the snake considered?

On one hand, this animal is associated with evil and considered a bearer of bad omens. For example, the proverb 佛口蛇心 (fó kǒu shé xīn, to have the mouth of a Buddha and the heart of a snake) which talks about "hiding evil intentions behind beautiful words", or the phrase 牛鬼蛇神 niú guǐ shé shén, which is used to describe all types of wicked people.

On the other hand, the snake has a positive image: the year of the snake is also called the year of the little dragon 小龙年 xiǎolóng nián, meaning that the snake is considered to be the little brother of the dragon, which is highly thought of in Chinese culture, so much so that it represents the Chinese people (the Chinese define themselves as 龙的传人, descendants of the dragon).

Therefore, the snake hasn't always represented evil in Chinese culture. Both Nüwa che Fuxi (the Adam and Eve of Chinese mythology) are often depicted to have the body of a snake from the waist down, just like the creator of the world according to "The Classic of Mountains and Seas" (山海经 Shānhǎi jīng) who had the face of a human and the body of a snake. For a long time, the snake was considered the symbol of the beginning of the world, until this figure became obscured by that of the dragon, a positive symbol of excellence in Chinese culture.

> **When is the next year of the snake? What are the characteristics of someone born under this sign? Do you know someone who was born in the year of the snake? Discuss with your friends in class.**

3. 对牛弹琴

▶ 4

　　春秋的时候，鲁国有个很有名的音乐家，他的名字叫公明仪。他很喜欢音乐。古筝、二胡、琵琶他都喜欢，但是他最喜欢弹琴。他弹琴弹得很好，大家都喜欢听他弹琴。

　　有一年的春天，他带着琴来到离城市很近的田野走走。田野的环境很舒服，很美。他很想找一个合适的地方弹琴放松放松。他到处看看，发现离他那儿不远的一个地方有一头牛正在吃草。他马上决定要对这头牛弹一首优美动听的曲子。

　　公明仪弹的曲子虽然悦耳动听，但是那头牛根本没有在听，仍然低着头继续吃草，不理会公明仪美丽的音乐。公明仪想，可能我弹的曲子不够好听，又对牛弹了他最好听的曲子，可是老牛仍然低着头继续吃草。

春秋 chūnqiū *Springs and Autumns* (period from 722 B.C. to 481 B.C.)
音乐家 yīnyuèjiā *musician*
古筝 gǔzhēng/二胡 èrhú/琵琶 pípá *traditional musical instruments*
弹 tán *to play (a stringed musical instrument)*
田野 tiányě *field*

曲子 qǔzi *piece of music*
继续 jìxù *to continue*
理会 lǐhuì *to look after, to pay attention to*
优美动听 yōuměi dòngtīng *melodious*
悦耳动听 yuè'ěr dòngtīng *pleasant to listen to*

公明仪觉得很无奈。他弹得很好听，但是那头不懂音乐的牛不会欣赏他的音乐。

过了一会儿他又想出了一个办法。他想，可能我弹的音乐太美丽，牛不喜欢，我试一个新的曲子吧。他开始弹不是曲子的音乐：他弹出一段奇怪杂乱的声音，有的像嗡嗡的蜻蜓声，有的像迷路的小牛发出的叫声。

这个时候，老牛甩了一下尾巴，离开了那块草地，去找新鲜的草吃。

那"对牛弹琴"是什么意思呢？

主要是说，你对一个什么都不懂的人说太深的话没有什么用，只会浪费你的时间！■

 你来猜！ Try to guess: what is the moral of this story? Is there a similar proverb in English?

无奈 wúnài *defenseless, unable*
欣赏 xīnshǎng *to appreciate*
杂乱 záluàn *untidy*
嗡嗡 wēng wēng *hum*
(onomatopoeic sound)

蜻蜓 qīngtíng *dragonfly*
甩 shuǎi *to swing, to shake*; 甩尾巴 shuǎi wěibā *to wag one's tail*
浪费 làngfèi *to waste*

语言点 A closer look

1 "他带<u>着</u>琴来到离城市很近的田野走走"
The aspect particle 着 zhe

We use the aspect particle 着 after the verb to indicate the continuation of the action or state indicated by the verb. In English we sometimes use the *-ing* form or we may add an adverb like *still*, or even a verb such as *to continue to*. A sentence with 着 often ends in the particle 呢.

- 外面下着雪。 It's snowing outside. (It's still snowing / It continues to snow) ≠ 外面下雪。
- 他穿着一条牛仔裤。 He's wearing a pair of jeans (he put them on and he continues to wear them) ≠ 他穿一条牛仔裤。

It can also be used to express the way in which an action of the second verb in the sentence is carried out with the structure V1 + 着 + V2.

- 他喜欢躺着看电视。 He likes watching TV lying down.
- 黎明听着音乐睡着了。 Li Ming falls asleep whilst watching TV.

2 "他到处看看，发现离他那儿不远的一个地方有一头牛<u>正在</u>吃草" **The adverb 正在 zhèngzài**

We use the adverb 正在 to indicate that the action of the verb (or the adjective which has the function of a verb) which follows is being carried out.

- 我正在看书，妈妈正在做饭。 I am reading, my mum is cooking.
- 老师正在改卷子，不能改你的作业。 The teacher is marking tests, he can't mark your homework.

The adverbs 正 and 在 can also be used to indicate that an action is being carried out, and they are interchangeable in many cases.

> 正在 highlights the action being carried out, while 着 underlines the continuation of the action.

Activities

练习

1 Match the picture with the word and find the most appropriate translation.

给下面的乐器选择对应的图案。

1 ☐ 二胡
2 ☐ 琵琶
3 ☐ 笛子
4 ☐ 锣
5 ☐ 古筝
6 ☐ 古琴
7 ☐ 大鼓
8 ☐ 波浪鼓

a
b
c
d
e
f
g
h

2 Dictation: Listen to the recording and write the story in Chinese.

听写练习：认真听录音，然后把故事用汉字写下来。

3 Describe the photo.

看图说故事。

4 Let's talk about you!

说说自己！

1 你喜欢唱歌吗？你唱过卡拉OK吗？
2 你觉得为什么卡拉OK在中国这么火？
3 你会弹什么乐器？
4 你认识哪些中国歌手？
5 你会唱中国歌吗？你想不想学？

Chinese music: past and present

古筝 Guzheng, 二胡 Erhu, 琵琶 Pipa are all traditional musical instruments used in traditional Chinese music and played by plucking their strings.

Traditional Chinese music, with the opening of China to the world during the seventies, has been influenced by and mixed with music from Western and other Asian countries, in particular music from Hong Kong (the so-called Cantopop, because it is sung in Cantonese), from Japan and from South Korea. Even if the music and the more 红 singers have changed over the years, in the music of the last decades one this prevails: the Chinese love of karaoke (卡拉OK, which we also see written as KTV). From the karaoke halls where you sang in front of everyone, which were made very popular in Hong Kong during the seventies, to the 迷你 KTV (places where you can sing and record your performance) present in all shopping centres, to the karaoke apps, it's almost impossible to find a Chinese person who has never in their life 点一首哥，唱个卡拉.

Did you know...?

In English we use one verb, *play*, with every single type of instrument, but in Chinese the verb changes according to how the instrument is played.

弹 (tán) is used for piano 钢琴 and other instruments with chords or strings, for example the guitar 吉他, the Pipa 琵琶 and the Guzheng 古筝.

拉 (lā) is used for instruments like the violin 小提琴, the viola 中提琴 and the cello 大提琴. Among the traditional instruments the Erhu 二胡 is used.

吹 (chuī) is used for wind instruments (it literally means *to blow*) like the flute 笛子, the clarinet 单簧管 and the traditional Sheng 笙.

打 (dǎ), which means *to hit*, is used for percussion instruments, 鼓 gǔ.

敲 (qiāo) is used for the gong, 锣 luó, and the triangle 三角铁. 敲 it translates as *to knock* or *to hit*. We also use it to talk about knocking on a door 敲门.

4. 血浓于水

我叫远航，我很喜欢这个名字。小时候，我问妈妈远航是什么意思，她说："是坐船去很远的地方的意思。世界很大，小航长大以后要离开家，去远方看看，知道吗？"我说："好啊，我们一家人一起去。"妈妈笑了笑说："你自己去吧，爸爸妈妈害怕坐飞机。"我觉得，爸妈除了"害怕"坐飞机以外，也没有时间去旅游，因为他们工作很忙。爸爸白天在工厂工作，晚上下班以后去当出租车司机，所以我很少看见他。可是他第二天早上回家的时候，经常给我买一些好吃的东西：鸡蛋、<u>蛋糕</u>、面条或者<u>水果</u>。妈妈在饭店当服务员，她每天上班以前，都会带我去坐公共汽车上学。<u>长大</u>以前，我没去过很远的地方，可是我也看到了外面的世界，因为爸妈有空就带我去图书馆，让我<u>读</u>很多有趣的故事。我在书里认识了很多<u>国家</u>和<u>城市</u>，

蛋糕 dàngāo *cake*
水果 shuǐguǒ *fruit*
长大 zhǎng dà *to grow, to grow up*

读 dú *to read, to attend*
国家 guójiā *state, country*
城市 chéngshì *city*

使我感到快乐，也使我爱上了旅游。读大学的时候，拿着护照和家里给我的零用钱，我去了很多地方，认识了很多新的朋友，也慢慢地明白了爸妈对我的爱。虽然他们没有很多时间照顾我，可是给了我好的生活环境，他们不是害怕坐飞机，而是把机会给了我。

血浓于水，爸妈能不爱自己的孩子吗？想到这儿，我眼睛红了。我把照相机放进行李箱，拿着买好的三张机票，坐上回家的火车。我决定送一份礼物给爸妈：用自己打工赚的钱带他们一起去旅游，看外面的世界。

 你来猜！ Try to guess: what is the moral of this story? Is there a similar proverb in English?

注意!

读: This character has three different meanings, two of which you have met in the story you just read. Can you find them?

读	*to read (aloud)* 学生都会读课文。
	All the students can read the text.
读//书	*to attend (a school, a course)* 我弟弟现在在读威尼斯大学。
	My younger brother attends a course at the University of Venice.
读	*to be read* 这个字你知道怎么读吗？
	Do you know how this character is read?

使 shǐ *to make something happen, to make sure something happens*
爱上 àishàng *to fall in love*
虽然 suīrán *in spite of, even if*

照顾 zhàogù *to take care of*
环境 huánjìng *environment*
浓 nóng *dense, concentrated*
赚钱 zhuàn qián *to earn*

语言点 A closer look

1 "我觉得，爸妈除了害怕坐飞机以外，也没有时间去旅游，因为他们工作很忙。"

The structure 除了。。。以外 chúle... yǐwài

The structure 除了。。。以外 is translated into *expect for* or *as well as...*

- 除了北京以外，我们还想去上海旅游。 We plan to visit Beijing as well as Shanghai.
- 罗明除了鱼以外，什么都喜欢吃。 Luo Ming likes all types of food, except for fish.

As you can see from the examples, this structure is made using 还 and 都.

2 "...看书<u>使</u>我感到快乐..." **The causative verb** 使 shǐ

The verb 使, along with 让, 叫 and 请 are causative verbs, which are used when the subject does not carry out an action directly, but makes a second subject carry out the action.

- subject 1 + causative verb + object / subject verb 2 +
  妈妈　　　　让　　　　　　儿子
  verb 2 (object)
  　去　中国学习汉语。
  The mother lets her son go to China to study Chinese.

- subject 1 + causative verb + object / subject verb 2 +
  他爸爸的话　　　使　　　　　　他
  psychological verb
  　很难过。
  His father's words made him upset.

- subject 1 + causative verb + object / subject verb 2 +
  跑步　　　(可以) 让　　　　　你
  predicate adjective
  　更健康。
  Running makes you healthier. (Running makes sure that you are in better health.)

> **Can you find the causative verb in the story "有志竟成"?** ....

29

怎么起个好的中文名字？**Chinese names and names in Chinese.**

Has anyone ever asked you to write their name in Chinese? As you know, English names (or foreign names in general) don't have an equivalent in Chinese. You can always suggest a "transcription" of the name in Chinese characters, but it will sound strange and foreign to a Chinese person. This transcription is used to transcript foreign names using characters: so 特朗普 would be Donald Trump, or 马可波罗 would be Marco Polo, but it would be very strange to introduce yourself as 阿拉尼斯•莫里赛特, if your name was Alanis Morisette.

For this reason, when you study Chinese or work with a Chinese organisation, sooner or later you will come across the question: 你的中文名字是什么？ Chinese names put the surname first (one character; there are very few formed of two characters), then the name (one or two characters). In general, surnames use limited characters, but first names can use any character.

There are essentially three approaches to choosing your Chinese name:
The **phonetic translation approach** (we "translate" the sound of our name): Young= Yang Linda = lin da → choose three characters with this pronunciation, used respectively as surname and name → 杨琳达.
The **semantic translation approach** (we "translate" the meaning of our name: Jade White → for White 白, for Jade 玉、琳、翠 or 碧 (characters which have these meanings).
The **mixed approach**: use both, one for the surname and one for the name.

We use both 起名 and 取名 to say *choose* or *give a name* in Chinese.

Translate this short text, then write a similar one which describes the origin of your Chinese name.

我的中文名字是我老公给我起的。我的名字叫雅丽，优雅的雅，美丽的丽。我老公为什么会起一个这么美丽的名字给我呢？他就是希望我会变成又优雅又美丽。很多父母起他们的孩子的名字的时候会把他们对孩子的希望放在他们的名字里。你父母为什么给你起那个名字呢？

Activities
练习

1 **Guess the meaning of the following words.**

猜猜生词的意思。

1 ☐ 害怕		**a**	to work
2 ☐ 白天		**b**	life
3 ☐ 零用钱		**c**	pocket money
4 ☐ 生活		**d**	to be frightened
5 ☐ 打工		**e**	in the daytime

▶ 5 **2 Dictation: Listen to the recording and write the story in Chinese.**

听写练习：认真听录音，然后把故事用汉字写下来。

3 Answer the following questions.

回答问题。

1 为什么远航的父母给他起了这个名字？
2 远航的父母害怕坐飞机吗？
3 远航小的时候是不是经常坐飞机去旅游？
4 他喜欢看书吗？为什么？
5 血浓于水这个成语是什么意思？

4 Let's talk about you!

说说自己！

1 你喜欢旅游吗？你去过哪些国家？
2 意大利人平时什么时候去旅游？
3 你的名字是什么意思？是谁给你起的？
4 你有没有中文名字？

5. 一举两得

　　春秋的时候，在一个偏远的山村里有一个勇敢的小伙子叫卞庄子。他长得又高大又聪明。有一天在离山村不远的森林里有两只老虎正在争吃一头黄牛。一个正在在森林里摘水果的人看到了马上回村里跟大家说："森林里有两只老虎，它们杀死了一头牛，现在两只都想吃，肯定会闹起来，咱们一起去看看吧！"卞庄子听到了消息以后就想，自己那么勇敢，应该上去捕杀两只老虎，保护村民的安全才对！他正准备过去的时候，站在旁边的老头突然跟他说："小伙子，老虎很凶猛，你一个人要想杀死两只老虎太危险了，很可能自己也会被老虎杀死。以我看来，这两只老虎争吃一头牛一定会吵架，到最后小老虎会咬伤

村 cūn *village*
勇敢 yǒnggǎn *brave*
卞庄子 Biàn Zhuāngzǐ *(first) name*
争吃 zhēngchī *to fight over food*
摘 zhāi *to pick (fruit, vegetables)*
杀 shā *to kill;* 杀死 shāsǐ *to kill making dying*

闹 nào *to make noise*
消息 xiāoxi *news*
正准备 zhèng zhǔnbèi *to be ready to, to prepare to do something*
以我看来 yǐ wǒ kàn lái *in my opinion*
吵架 chǎo jià *to argue*
咬 yǎo *to bite*

大老虎，大老虎会咬死小老虎。那时你再上去杀老虎不是更安全吗？"小伙子一听就觉得老头子说的话很有<u>道理</u>，所以就开始在旁边等。等什么呢？就等两只老虎<u>打</u>完<u>架</u>。果然不久两只老虎就打了起来，大虎咬死了小虎，自己也伤痕累累，筋疲力尽。这时年轻人提着剑<u>冲</u>了上去，杀死了大老虎。

　　一举两得这句话的意思就是从这个故事而来的：<u>付</u>出一份的努力却能得到两份的回报。

 你来猜！ Try to guess: what is the moral of this story? Is there a similar proverb in English?

有道理 yǒu dàolǐ *to be reasonable*
打架 dǎ jià *to have a fist-fight*
冲 chōng *to rush*
付 fù *to spend, to pay*

筋疲力尽 jīnpí lìjìn *without any strength*
伤痕累累 shānghénlěilěi *covered in wounds*

语言点 A closer look

1 "那时你再<u>上去</u>杀老虎不是更安全吗？"
Simple direction complements

We form a simple direction complement with a verb of motion + 来 or 去. It indicates that the action of the main verb is carried out near to the speaker (main verb + 来) or far from the speaker (main verb + 去).

- 你<u>上来</u>吧！ Go up! *the speaker is already "up" (Come up!)
- 你<u>上去</u>吧！ Go up! *the speaker is still "down" (Go up!)
- "你几点<u>回来</u>吃饭？" "我今天要加班，不<u>回去</u>吃饭。" "What time are you coming back to eat?" "I have to do overtime today, I'm not coming back to eat".

The verbs of motion most widely used with this structure are 上/下, 进/出, 回, 过.

When the object indicates a place, it is always positioned between the main verb and 去/来.

- 我<u>进</u>商店<u>去</u>。 I go into the shop.
- 下课以后，我<u>回家去</u>。 When I finish the lesson, I go home.

2 "这时年轻人提着剑<u>冲了上去</u>"
Compound direction complements

A compound direction complement is made up of a verb of movement, which indicates the way in which the movement is carried out, + one of the motion verbs (上/下, 进/出, 回, 过, 起) + 来 or 去.

- 老师叫我们把书<u>拿出来</u>。 The teacher told us to take out our books.
- 他突然冲<u>进</u>教室<u>来</u>。 He suddenly rushed to the classroom.
- 我已经把你的衣服<u>放</u>进箱子里<u>去</u>了。 I've already put your clothes in the suitcase.

3 "肯定会闹<u>起来</u>" Figurative use of direction complements

Some direction complements have a more figurative use, which goes beyond their literal meaning. Amongst the most common we often see 起来.

- "你记得阿明的电话号码吗？" "我想不<u>起来</u>。" "Do you remember A-ming's telephone number?" "I can't bring it to mind."
- 臭豆腐闻<u>起来</u>很臭，吃<u>起来</u>很香！ Strong-smelling tofu smells bad when you take a sniff, but it's delicious to eat!

What is the meaning of 起来 in the story?

....

Activities

练习

//

1 **Find the resultative verbs in the story and write a sentence using each one. (minimum 5)**

把故事里的结果补语都找出来，然后用来造句子。(五个以上)

▶ 6 **2** **Dictation: Listen to the recording and write the story in Chinese.**

听写练习：认真听录音，然后把故事用汉字写下来。

3 **Describe the picture.**

看图说故事。

Talk about when you
一举两得！

4 **Let's talk about you!**

说说自己！

1 你学了几年的汉语？
2 你为什么开始学习汉语？
3 你觉得学汉语怎么样？为什么？
4 你认为汉字背起来难不难？
5 英语和汉语比起来哪个难学？

注意 !

冲 chōng has many uses and meanings, and you will use one of these often in China; look at the photo and guess which one it is.

36

6. 塞翁失马

战国时期有一位老人，他的名字叫塞翁。他养了许多马，有一天马群中突然有一匹马走失了。

塞翁的邻居们听到这件事以后，都去他家安慰他，跟他说不必太着急，年龄已经大了，要多注意身体。塞翁见有那么多人关心他，笑笑地说："丢了一匹马损失不大，没准还会带来福气。"

邻居听了塞翁的话，心里觉得好笑。马丢了，明明是件坏事，他却认为也许是好事，可能老头是自我安慰而已。可是过了几天，走失的马不仅自己回家，还带了一匹骏马回来。

邻居听说马自己回来了，非常佩服塞翁的预见，跟塞翁说："还是您老有远见，马不仅没有丢，还带回一匹好马，真是福气呀。"

塞翁听了邻居的祝贺，一点都不高兴："白白得了一匹好马，不一定是什么福气，也许会带来麻烦。"

塞翁 Sàiwēng (first) name
养 yǎng to raise
失 shī to lose
邻居 línjū neighbours
安慰 ānwèi to comfort
着急 zháo jí to worry, to be worries
损失 sǔnshī loss

没准 méizhǔn it doesn't mean that, probably, maybe
也许 yěxǔ perhaps
佩服 pèifú to admire
祝贺 zhùhè to congratulate, congratulations

37

邻居们觉得塞翁越老越怪，明明心里要高兴，他仍然<u>有意</u>不说出来。

塞翁有个独生子，非常喜欢骑马。他发现带回来的那匹马是匹好马，他每天都骑马出游。一天，他从马背上<u>跌</u>下来，<u>摔断</u>了腿。

邻居一听就到塞翁的家慰问。塞翁说："没什么，腿摔断了却保住性命，还算是福气呢。"邻居们觉得他又在胡言乱语。他们真不明白，摔断腿还能算什么福气。

不久，<u>匈奴</u>　<u>入侵</u>，<u>青年人</u>应征入伍，塞翁的儿子因为摔断了腿，不能去当<u>兵</u>。<u>战争</u>结束了，入伍的青年都死了，<u>唯有</u>塞翁的儿子保住了性命。到最后，好事变成了坏事，坏事<u>倒</u>变成了好事，这就是塞翁失马这句成语的意思。　■

你来猜！ Try to guess: what is the moral of this story? Is there a similar proverb in English?

有意 yǒuyì *on purpose*
跌 diē *to fall*
摔断 shuāiduàn *to break*
匈奴 xiōngnú *Huns (people)*
入侵 rùqīn *to invade*
青年人 qīngniánrén *youth, guy*
兵 bīng *soldier*

战争 zhànzhēng *war*
唯有 wéiyǒu *alone*
倒 dào *on the contrary*
胡言乱语 húyán luànyǔ *to talk nonsense*
应征入伍 yìngzhēng rùwǔ *to be called up to do military service*

语言点 A closer look

1 "马不仅没有丢，还带回一匹好马"
The structure 不仅。。。还 。。。bùjǐn... hái...

The structure 不仅。。。还 。。。 is translated in English as *not only... but also,* and it can replace 不但。。。而且。。。 In place of 而且 and 还 we may also find 也.

In both sentences, the subject must be the same, and it is expressed just once at the beginning of the sentence.

- 他不但很聪明，而且很帅。 He is not only intelligent, but also very good-looking.
- 那个小食店的菜不仅卖得很便宜，还非常好吃！ That small restaurant has great prices, and their food is delicious too!
- 我们的老师不仅汉语说得很好，还会说广州话！ Our teacher not only speaks Mandarin really well, but he also knows Cantonese.

2 "有一天马群中突然有一匹马走失了" and "心里明明要高兴，他仍然有意不说出来"
Adverbs and adjectives with 然 rán

The suffix 然 is often used in Chinese to make adverbs or adjectives with two syllables, which indicate the state of the subject. The meaning of a word formed like this comes from the first character.

突然 suddenly, unexpectedly, sudden, unexpected
- 他的孩子突然哭了起来。 His son suddenly started to cry.
- 这个消息太突然了。 This is really unexpected news.

仍然 (used mainly in the written form) still
- 我的美国朋友，回国以后仍然和我们保持联系。 My American friend still stays in touch with us, even after returning to his home country.

- 这条法律仍然有效。 This law is no longer valid.

当然 certain, certainly, naturally
- "你明天跟我们一起去上课吗？" "当然去！" "Are you coming to the lesson with us tomorrow?" "I certainly am!"
- 你考上HSK6级是当然的! It's sure you will manage to pass the HSK6!

虽然 although, despite, even if (often followed by 但是, 可是)

- 马可虽然没有去过中国，但是他汉语的发音非常标准。 Even if Mark has never been to China, his Chinese pronunciation is perfect.
- 欣欣虽然还小，可是已经会做家务了。 Although Xinxin is still only young, she already knows how to do housework.

既然 since, because, given that 既然 + the fact, 那/就。。。

- 小桁，你既然生病了，就别去上学了！ Xiao Heng, given that you're feeling unwell, don't go to school.
- 既然你没买到票，我只能一个人去看演唱会了。 Because you didn't manage to get a ticket, I have to go to the concert alone.

显然 obviously, clearly

- 新开的服装店的价钱显然太贵了。 The new clothes shop which has just opened is obviously too expensive.
- 显然，你昨天晚上没睡够觉，你的熊猫眼也太明显了！ You obviously didn't sleep enough last night. Your panda-eyes are very visible.

Do you know others? ....
....

3 "邻居们觉得塞翁越老越怪"
The structure 越。。。越。。。 yuè... yuè...

越 + action verb / predicative adjective + 越 + predicative adjective.

- 真美慕她，她越吃越瘦！ I envy her so much; the more she eats the slimmer she gets.
- 汉字不难学，学得越多越容易记。 Chinese characters aren't so difficult to study; the more you learn the easier they are to remember. This structure is similar to the structure 越来越 + ADJ, which can be traduced as *more and more* or *the more time goes by, the more...*
- 她养的狗越来越听话。 The dog that he is training is becoming more and more obedient.
- 你的汉语越来越好，你一定要继续努力！ Your Chinese is getting better every day; you should keep up the good work!

Activities
练习

1 Guess the meaning of the following words.

猜猜生词的意思。

1 ☐ 不必		**a**	to finish
2 ☐ 丢		**b**	forecast
3 ☐ 预见		**c**	to be unnecessary
4 ☐ 远见		**d**	foresight
5 ☐ 白白得		**e**	to become
6 ☐ 性命		**f**	life
7 ☐ 结束		**g**	to lose
8 ☐ 变成		**h**	without strength

注意 !

Apart from the meanings *white* and *light*, that you already know, 白 can also be used as an adverb with two very distinct meanings.

- 我等了她半天她都没来，我白去了一趟。 I waited for her for half a day and she didn't come. I went there for nothing.
- 那件衬衫太难看了，你白给我我也不要。 That blouse is really awful, I wouldn't want it even if you were giving it to me for free.

2 Dictation: Listen to the recording and write the story in Chinese.

听写练习：认真听录音，然后把故事用汉字写下来。

3 Answer the following questions.

回答问题。

1 塞翁丢了马为什么不着急？
2 邻居觉得塞翁怎么样？
3 塞翁的儿子喜欢做什么？
4 塞翁的儿子为什么没去当兵？
5 到最后你觉得丢了马是不是好事？为什么？

4 Translate, and form sentences with the following adjectives.

翻译以下形容词，然后造句子。

1	好吃	5	好学	9	难记
2	好听	6	难喝	10	难得
3	好做	7	难闻		
4	好玩	8	难看		

> **Before a verb, 好 can have two meanings. What are they?**
> ....

5 Put the sentences in order.

连词成句。

1 请·他家·唱歌·很多·到·里·吃烧烤·他
了·朋友
2 马拉松·我·是·参加·男朋友·今天·第一次
3 她·带·来到·玩儿·足球·星期六·着
新买的·公园里
4 姐姐·喜欢·去·非常·以外·还·喜欢·旅游
除了·打排球·我
5 被·她·的·了·蛋糕·做·小妹妹·吃完

缘分和命运: **The concept of destiny**

缘分 and 命运 can both be translated with the word *destiny*, but these two words don't have the same meaning in Chinese.

缘分 (yuánfèn) refers to the destiny which binds two people, destined to meet and share part of their lives together. We walk about 缘分 between husband and wife, and also between friends or even perfect strangers who sit together on a plane.

命运 (mìngyùn) indicates the pre-written path that a person walks in his life, and it refers to every aspect of this.

Look at the following sentences:

- 死生命也 in classic Chinese is attributed to Zhuanzi and means: "life and death depend on your destiny", if the 命运 dictates that your life goes a certain way, you can't change it.

- 有缘千里来相会，无缘对面不相逢。 If it is destined to be, you will find each other even if you are a thousand *li* apart. If it is not destined to be you will not see each other even if you find yourselves stood facing one another.

- 有缘无份 "To have fate but not destiny" refers to those couples who were destined to meet but were never destined to stay together. It is often used when one of the two wants to leave the relationship.

- 一命、二运、三风水、四积功德、五读书。 This is the first part of a saying which lists, in fifteen points, the most important things in the life of a person. Can you name them?

....

7. 九牛一毛

▶8

　　西汉时代有个很有名的大将军名叫李陵，他非常勇敢，而且骑马、射箭都是他的强项。因为匈奴经常入侵他的国家，他奉汉武帝的命令，带领军队去攻打匈奴。可惜的是，他的军队士兵很少，所以他不得不投降。

　　武帝听到这件事以后非常生气，他觉得李陵不但没能立下大功，还轻易对敌人投降，所以决定把李陵的家人都杀了。

　　其它大臣们也对李陵有很大意见，只有司马迁觉得李陵已经尽力而为，还跟大家说："李陵将军每次带兵都有很好的成绩，只有这一次，他没有得到别的将军的协助，而且他的步兵比匈奴的少得多，但他还继续抗战，还杀伤了一

将军 jiāngjūn *general*
李陵 Lǐ Líng *(first) name*
勇敢 yǒnggǎn *brave*
射箭 shèjiàn *archery*
强项 qiángxiàng *strong point*
奉(命令) fèng mìnglìng *to accept (orders from a superior)*
汉武帝 Hànwǔ dì *Emperor Hanwu*
带领 dàilǐng *to conduct*
军队 jūnduì *army*
攻打 gōngdǎ *to attack*

投降 tóuxiáng *to surrender, surrender*
敌人 dírén *enemy*
大臣 dàchén *official, civil servant*
对(某人)有意见 duì (mǒu rén) yǒu yìjiàn *to find something funny about someone*
协助 xiézhù *to receive help*
立下大功 lìxià dàgōng *to get a great result*
尽力而为 jìnlì érwéi *to do your very best*

万多敌兵，一直到粮草都用完了，才不得不投降，这样的战绩大概没有几个人能做得到，李陵实在是个了不起的将领啊！"

汉武帝听到司马迁为李陵辩解特别生气，马上下令把司马迁打进监狱。司马迁好几次都想自杀，可是他想到自己这样死去，就像是九头牛身上少了一根毛那样，没有人会知道。所以，他下定决心，勇敢地活下去，最后终于完成了《史记》这部名流千古的历史书。

最初的"九牛亡一毛"这句话变成了"九牛一毛"的四字成语，意思是某种东西，甚至人才都只是整体的一部分，就好像九头牛身上的一根毛一样，没有什么价值。

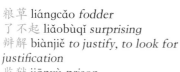

你来猜！ Try to guess: what is the moral of this story? Is there a similar proverb in English?

粮草 liángcǎo *fodder*
了不起 liǎobùqǐ *surprising*
辩解 biànjiě *to justify, to look for justification*
监狱 jiānyù *prison*
下定决心 xiàdìng juéxīn *to decide, to be determined*

终于 zhōngyú *in the end, finally*
部分 bùfen *part*
价值 jiàzhí *value*
名流千古 míngliú qiāngǔ *famous through the centuries*

语言点 A closer look

1 "他的军队士兵很少，所以他<u>不得不</u>投降"
The expression 不得不 bùdébù

We can translate this expression as "can't not" o "can't do without (doing) something". Other similar expressions are 不能不 and 只好. They are all used before the verb.

- 你不得不承认，她写的字比你的好看多了。You can't deny (not admit) that the characters that she writes are much more beautiful that the ones that you write.
- 现在到处打特价，我不得不去逛街买新衣服。There are sales all over right now; I can't not go and buy myself some new clothes.

2 "这样的战绩大概没有几个人能做<u>得</u>到"
The potential complement with 得 dé

The potential complement expresses the possibility of an action, given by verb 1, to reach the result expressed by verb 2:

affirmative sentence   sogg + verb 1 + 得 + verb 2
negative sentence   sogg + verb 1 + 不 + verb 2

- 你能看得懂汉字吗？ Are you able to read (and understand) Chinese characters?
  * 看懂 is a resultative verb
- 这么贵的鞋子你能买得起吗？ Can you afford such expensive shoes?
  The verb 起 as a resultative indicates the economic (but not only economic) possibility to achieve verb 1.
- 那条路太窄，我这辆货车一定进不去。 That road is to narrow; my truck won't be able to go through.
- 他的名字太奇怪了，我总是记不住。 His name is too strange; I can never remember it.

看不起 has a particular figurative use, and means "look from top to bottom" or "not consider (something, someone) good enough".

- 我家里穷，大家都看不起我。 I come from a poor family; no one thinks I'm good enough.

3 "一直到粮草都用完了，**才**不得不投降"

The use of 才 cái

The adverb 才 can be translated into English in different ways.

- *Just/only*, when it is followed by a quantity:
  现在才六点，你为什么这么早起床？ It's only six o'clock, why are you up so early?
- *Only then*, when it is followed by a verb:
  他明年才能去中国。 Only next year will be he able to go to China. *
  In this case, the action happens later than anticipated.
- *Only after*, when acting as a connector between two verbs, one of which follows the other (only when the first action is complete, does the second one occur):
  他要大学毕业才能出国留学。 He can go abroad to study only after he graduates.

* To show that an action happens before it was anticipated, we can use 就.
他明年就能去中国。 He can go to China as soon as next year.

4 "他下定决心，勇敢地活下去"

The figurative use of direction complements

As we have already seen, some direction complements also have a more figurative use, which differs from its literal use.
Here are a few examples of the figurative use of 下去 meaning *to continue*.

- 我看下去吧，故事还很长呢。 Carry on reading! The story is still very long.
- 这首歌太难听了，我听不下去。 This song is terrible, I just can't go on listening to it.
- 你再这样吃下去，就穿不了新买的衣服。 If you continue to eat like that, you'll not be able to fit into your new dress.

注意 ❗

How do we read 了 in 穿不了?

....

49

司马迁和他的史记
Sima Qian and the Shiji

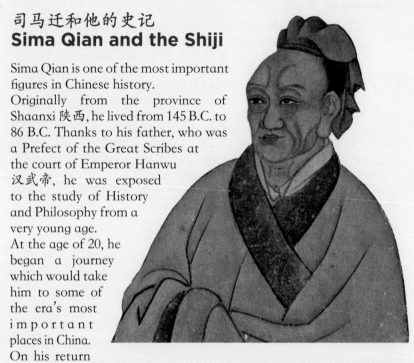

Sima Qian is one of the most important figures in Chinese history.

Originally from the province of Shaanxi 陕西, he lived from 145 B.C. to 86 B.C. Thanks to his father, who was a Prefect of the Great Scribes at the court of Emperor Hanwu 汉武帝, he was exposed to the study of History and Philosophy from a very young age.

At the age of 20, he began a journey which would take him to some of the era's most important places in China.

On his return from that journey, he was nominated as Palace Attendant: thanks to this assignment he was sent to the West following a military expedition against the Xiongnu barbarians 匈奴, from which he returned almost immediately to carry out and finish the research work which his father, Sima Tan, had begun. In 109 B.C., he began writing the Shiji 史记, *Records of the Grand Historian*, and he became Court Historian and Advisor to the Emperor.

The episode which is documented in history is a real account of events: In 99 B.C., Sima Qian was sentenced to death (a punishment subsequently changed to castration) for defending General Li Ling, conquered and captured by Xiongnu, and from whom he had requested asylum. On his release from prison, rather than committing suicide, in accordance with the custom of the time, he decided to go on living, to give himself some time to finish the Shiji, which became, in form and content, the reference point for future historians, both in and beyond China. The work of 130 chapters, divided into annals, charts, treaties, genealogies and biographies reports the events of the time of the Yellow Emperor (2600 B.C. circa) until the writer's lifetime.

Activities

练习

///

1 史记 **is divided into five parts. Guess the meaning of the following words.**

猜猜生词的意思。

1 ☐ genealogy		a	表
2 ☐ chart		b	本纪
3 ☐ biography		c	书
4 ☐ treaty		d	列传
5 ☐ annal		e	世家

▶ 8 **2 Dictation: Listen to the recording and write the story in Chinese.**

听写练习：认真听录音，然后把故事用汉字写下来。

3 Answer the following questions.

回答问题。

1 李陵是谁？他人怎么样？
2 他为什么打败不了匈奴？
3 汉武帝为什么对李陵有很大的意见？
4 为什么司马迁出狱以后没有自杀？
5 你会用汉语解释这句成语的意思吗？

4 Find the potential complements and resultative complements in the text and make sentences.

把故事里的可能补语和结果补语都找出来，
然后用来造句子。

....
....
....

8. 入乡随俗

▶9

很久以前，有一个地方，哪里的人都不喜欢穿衣服，所以这个地方叫"裸乡"。

一次，有一对兄弟去裸乡做生意。弟弟说："今日我们来到了裸乡，这里的人的习惯有点奇怪，是一个比较落后的地方。我们在这里，和他们交流起来比较困难。所以，我们应该遵循他们本地人的规矩。和他们相处的时侯，心态要柔和，语言要谦虚。我们还是一起进去吧！"哥哥说："还是你先进去看一下，之后回来告诉我具体情况。"弟弟答应了。

十天后，弟弟回来告诉哥哥："不管怎么样，必须要遵守当地的习俗。"哥哥就回答："他们都不穿衣服！你能接受他们这个怪习惯，我可不行！"

弟弟一个人又回到裸乡。他遵守那里的风俗，和当地人打成一片。

落后 luòhòu under-developed, old-fashioned
交流 jiāoliú to communicate, to interface
遵循 zūnxún to respect, to obey (a law)
相处 xiāngchǔ to have something to do with

柔和 róuhé sweet (natured)
谦虚 qiānxū humble, modest
具体 jùtǐ precise, specific
答应 dāying to give one's word
打成一片 dǎchéngyīpiàn to become one, to integrate

国王很喜欢他，国民也非常敬重他，他在裸乡做生意很成功。

哥哥看到弟弟成功决定也要去裸乡做生意，但是他没有像弟弟那样，按照那里的习惯去做而且总是说当地人不对，这里不行，那里不行，让他们觉得很不高兴。国王非常生气，国民也特别讨厌他。有人还抢了他的商品最后国王还想赶他出国，要弟弟求情，才能避免更大灾难。两兄弟离开裸乡的时候，裸乡的人民很热情地告别弟弟，对哥哥的态度却一点都不热情。哥哥很生气，非常恨弟弟。他想，他们为什么对你这么好，对我这么不好呢？肯定是你说我不好。于是对弟弟说："从今天以后，我们就不是兄弟了！"

入乡随俗的意思是到一个地方，就要顺从当地的习俗。

你来猜！ Try to guess: what is the moral of this story? Is there a similar proverb in English?

敬重 jìngzhòng *to appreciate*
讨厌 tǎo yàn *to hate*
求情 qiú qíng *to beg*

避免 bìmiǎn *to avoid*
顺从 shùncóng *to obey*

语言点 A closer look

1 "你能接受他们这个怪习惯，我<u>可</u>不行！"
The adverb 可 kě

Used as an adverb, 可 adds emphasis to the sentence.

- 你妹妹可漂亮！ Your younger sister is really beautiful.
- 今天外面特别冷，你可要穿够衣服啊！ It's really cold outside today, you really have to wrap up well.
- 大家说她做的蛋糕最好吃，我可不这么想。 Everyone says that her cakes are the tastiest, but I don't really agree.
- 她想去的这所大学我可没听说过。 I have absolutely never heard of the university she wants to go to.

> **注意！**
>
> 那可不! can be used like a question tag in English, (isn't it?, aren't you?, etc.) used to express agreement with the previous statement.

2 "裸乡的人民很热情地告别弟弟，对哥哥的态度<u>却</u>一点都不热情。"
The use of 却 què

The adverb 却 is used after the subject of an opposing sentence, to mean *however, but*.

- 她努力学习却没有考上大学。 He worked really hard on his studies however, he didn't manage to get into university.
- 他父母都会说汉语，她却一点儿都不会！ Both her parents speak Chinese, but she doesn't even speak it a little.

中国：一国多语，一国多族 China, a country of ethnic and linguistic minorities.

When you think of China, 普通话 and 汉 immediately spring to mind. But have you ever seen a Chinese person with blond hair and blue eyes? If you go to the autonomous province of Xinjiang Uigur, you could indeed meet one! Few people are aware of the ethnicities and languages which coexist in this country: in fact, it recognises 56 different ethnic minorities and there are almost 300 different languages spoken in China. The official language is Mandarin, but on a local level are also recognised other local languages: Tibetan in Tibet, Mongolian in Inner Mongolia, Uyghur in Xinjiang, Cantonese in Hong Kong and Macao, together with English and Portuguese. In many border areas, where different Chinese ethnic minorities live, and in many different autonomous counties, Vietnamese, Korean, Kyrgyz and Burmese are also spoken.

Cantonese is the most widely spoken variant of Chinese, both in China and around the world, thanks to the mass emigration towards the United States and Southeast Asia, which originated from the Guangdong province in the 19th Century.

The different languages and minorities which characterise the Chinese people are also well represented on the *Renminbi* banknotes.

The writing 中国人民银行 is written in *pinyin*, in printed capitals, as well as Mongolian, Tibetan, Uyghur Zhuang. (respectively from left to right, from top to bottom).

Ethnic minorities are represented on 1 *jiao* and 5 *jiao* banknotes.

Activities
练习

<hr>

1 **Guess the meaning of the following words.**

猜猜生词的意思。

1	☐ 裸乡		**a**	difficulty
2	☐ 生意		**b**	to hate
3	☐ 困难		**c**	calamity
4	☐ 规矩		**d**	to squash
5	☐ 情况		**e**	nudist village
6	☐ 遵守		**f**	business
7	☐ 赶		**g**	situation
8	☐ 灾难		**h**	rules
9	☐ 恨		**i**	to respect

▶ 9 **2** **Dictation: Listen to the recording and write the story in Chinese.**

听写练习：认真听录音，然后把故事用汉字写下来。

3 **Let's broaden our horizons!**

我们扩大知识！

1 Which Chinese ethnic minorities do you know? Where are they based?

2 Why are English and Portuguese, along with Cantonese, the official languages of Hong Kong and Macao?

3 Which are the most widely spoken dialects/languages amongst the Chinese community on the U.K.? Why?

4 Look at the political map, identify the countries which border with China and write the areas where these languages are spoken: Cantonese, Tibetan, Mongolian, Korean, Kyrgyz, Portuguese, English, Wu, Minnan, Xiang, Hakka, Zhuang.

9. 百闻不如一见

　　西汉汉武帝在位的时候羌族经常侵入汉朝国境。匈奴也想联合羌人共同侵略汉朝。汉武帝想削弱他们的实力就派人去攻打羌人，但是都失败了。到了汉宣帝当皇帝的时候，羌人更加肆无忌惮地侵略汉朝的边境。面对这种情况，已经七十多岁的老将赵充国自告奋勇地要到前线和羌人打上一仗，很多大臣看他那么老就觉得不太合适，还忙着跟汉宣帝说最好派别人去。汉宣帝也很担忧，不想让他去。赵充国就对他说："陛下，这场战争我去是最合适的了。"

　　汉宣帝反问他。"那将军要怎么攻打羌人呢？你估计羌人的实力怎么样？我们又该派多少将士去攻打他们呢？"　赵充国回答他："羌人的事，听别人说一百次也不如亲眼看见一次。对方军事力量的情况怎么样，我们在后方很难准确地估

在位 zàiwèi *to be in office*
羌族 qiāngzú *Qiang ethnic group*
侵入 qīnrù *to invade*
侵略 qīnlüè *to invade, to attack*
削弱 xuēruò *to weaken*
派 pài *to send an envoy*

担忧 dānyōu *to worry*
亲眼 qīnyǎn *with one's own eyes*
准确 zhǔnquè *precise*
肆无忌惮 sìwújìdàn *careless, reckless*
自告奋勇 zìgào fènyǒng *to volunteer to take on a difficult task*

计。"让我上前线了解，了解情况以后再来制定策略吧。"

汉宣帝点点头答应了他。赵充国率领了不到一万的骑兵，很快得离开了京城，巧妙地渡过了黄河，修筑城墙堡垒，部队就留在那儿，做好战斗准备。

他不停观察地形，了解羌人的情况，很快制定出作战的计划。他命令汉军不准出城攻击羌人。命令将士在边境开荒种地，减轻住在那里的百姓的负担，同时他还招降其他被胁迫的羌人部落，打算从内部打破羌人联合的计划，瓦解羌人的战斗主力。

赵充国的对敌策略和作战计划很快就起作用了。不久，朝廷就派兵平定了羌人的入侵,安定了西北边疆。百闻不如一见这句成语就是这个故事而来的。 ∎

 你来猜！Try to guess: what is the moral of this story? Is there a similar proverb in English?

策略 cèlüè *strategy, tactic*
率领 shuàilǐng *to conduct*
城墙堡垒 chéngqiáng bǎolěi *fortification walls*
开荒种地 kāihuāng zhòngdì *to reclaim*

负担 fùdān *responsibility, duty*
胁迫 xiépò *to force, to obligate*
部落 bùluò *tribe*
瓦解 wǎjiě *to disintegrate*
朝廷 cháotíng *imperial court*

成语和数字成语 Numbers and *chengyu*

How many *chengyu* exist? Some sources say that there are more than 30,000 *chengyu*, but far fewer are actually used in everyday life!

One thing is certain and that is that almost all the *chengyu* are made up of four characters, respecting the Chinese tendency and tradition for parallelism and symmetry. There are a few made up of three, five, up to a maximum of sixteen characters.

Every *chengyu* has a specific meaning in Chinese and can have many different functions within a sentence; it may be used as a subject, or a complement.

Most of the *chengyu* come from stories passed down from ancient times, and for this reason the terminology used in the *chengyu* is not commonly used in modern Chinese. In modern Chinese, the use of *chengyu* allows you to give a certain tone to a sentence, to make it sound less flat and certainly more sophisticated. Many companies use the *chengyu* when they advertise their products, often changing a character with a homophone, therefore adapting the *chengyu* to the advertised product.

The *chengyu* can be grouped in different ways, for example according to the number of characters, according to their use, or their origin, to the words they contain or the format of their structure. Let's look at some which relate to numbers:

不三不四	neither meat, nor fish
四面八方	everywhere
五颜六色	multicoloured
七嘴八舌	lit. seven mouths, eight tongues = very noisy because everyone wants to speak
七七八八	do things by halves (70/80%)
一刀两断	have a clean break
千变万化	continuous change
万众一心	everyone has the same opinion

We can see two different structures in these proverbs:

The format ABAB, where A is always a number, while B are words with the same meaning or of the same type (or vice versa); the format AABB, where the two As and the two Bs are the same or similar to each other.

一传十，十传百   *which spreads quickly*

In this proverb the format is ABA, ABA.

There is a game which helps you to practise the *chengyu* you have learned: 成语接龙, which can be translated as "Chain of proverbs". The rules of the game are easy: a player says a *chengyu* and the next player must say a proverb which begins with the last character, and so on. The record is a chain of 1500 proverbs... imagine that!

汉语怎么说？How do we say in Chinese?

成语大部分是从古代典籍而来的，跟现代汉语来比有很大不同。其中有古书上的成语，也有从古人文章中压缩而成的词组，还有一些是从人民口里常说的习用语而来的。有些成语的意思一看字面就可以理解，还有一些从字面上很不容易理解。成语是一种现成的话，跟习用语、谚语相近，但是还是有所不同。最主要的一点是习用语和谚语属于口语性质，成语属于书面语性质。其次成语几乎都是固定的四字结构，字面不能随意更换。习用语和谚语反而有一定的弹性，字可多可少，不限于四个。成语一般都是四字格式，不是四字的较少。成语的结构是多种多样的，在语言表达中有生动简洁、形象鲜明的作用。很多成语都有数字，有些很简单，有些很难，我们先来学一些一目了然的数字成语吧！

"一干二净"就是很干净的意思。"一清二楚"就是很清楚的意思，"千变万化"就是很多变化的意思，"千辛万苦"就是很辛苦的意思。那你猜猜五颜六色是什么意思呢？

有些数字成语会给你一个画面比如"七嘴八舌"就是七张嘴巴，八个舌头，很多人一起说话所以很吵的意思。还有"一传十十传百"指的是一个人告诉十个人，十个人告诉一百个人，也就是消息传得很快的意思。

还有一些数字成语看起来简单，但是不容易明白它的含义，比如"三三两两"是两个人三个人一起走，跟"三五成群"一样的意思。"七七八八"就是事情做了七成或八成，快要完成的意思。"一五一十"就是把事情从头到尾一清二楚的说出来的意思。"一日三秋"的意思是不能跟一个人见面的时候，时间过得很慢，慢得一天像三年那么长。

很多公司的广告里也能出现成语：某个冰箱公司的广告语是"领'鲜'一步"。他们把原本的"领先一步"的"先"字改成"鲜"字，因为这两个字是谐音。这样又说明自己的冰箱比其他牌子的冰箱更优秀，又体现了冰箱的作用，真是一举两得！

Activities
练习

1 **Guess the meaning of the following words.**
猜猜生词的意思。

1	☐ 陛下	**a**	to cheer up
2	☐ 反问	**b**	to ask (in answer to a question)
3	☐ 渡过	**c**	height
4	☐ 攻击	**d**	to lose
5	☐ 减轻	**e**	to attack
6	☐ 失败	**f**	to cross

▶ 10 **2** **Dictation: Listen to the recording and write the story in Chinese.**
听写练习：认真听录音，然后把故事用汉字写下来。

3 **Complete the crossword with Chinese proverbs.**
成语填字游戏。

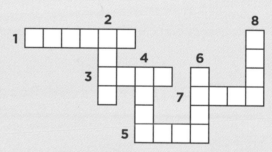

Across

1 The one where you're a little like Saint Thomas.

3 The one with the needle in a haystack.

5 The one where blood is not water.

7 The one where you're like brothers.

Down

2 The one where you have as many lives as a cat.

4 The one where you hit your opponent on the first attempt.

6 The one where you're as calm as tranquil sea.

8 The one with too much of a good thing.

Syllabus

语言点

中国成语故事 - Stories of Chinese Proverbs includes 9 stories from traditional Chinese proverbs. After each story, the reader will find a more in-depth linguistic analysis and/or cultural analysis in the "Culture talk" section, and a series of practice activities which relate to the story.

The syllabus of the linguistic examination HSK 2 is the main reference point for the texts. However, some vocabulary and structures have been added from the higher level of the HSK qualification.

These grammatical structures are dealt with in the "A closer look" sections.

New vocabulary, including names and place names, is highlighted only the first time they occur.

The main grammatical structures presented in this text are:

- Resultative verbs
- Direction verbs (simple and compound)
- The aspect particle 着
- Sentences with 把
- The 是。。。的 structure
- The particles 得 and 地
- The adverbs 正在, 在

 Chinese Graded Readers   HSK2-3
